*alone and embarrassed. Linda's tips include ones I may read to my family and friends who have told me to 'buck up.' Linda reveals her heart in two short anecdotes about her healing and now helps others with her coaching."*

**L.H.** from La Mesa, CA

*"The book is extremely helpful in promoting the individual's involvement in his or her own self care and continued recovery and improvement."*

**Mark D. Wiederhold, M.D., Ph.D., FACP**
President, The Virtual Reality Medical Center

*"I really appreciated reading your 121 tips. Thank you for that!!! I have not met someone like me in this town and sometimes I feel so lonely. I want to write with someone so compassionate as you. I think you really understand me."*

**Caroline Jane Cooke** from Panama

*"I applaud Linda for sharing her own knowledge and personal experiences living with panic and anxiety in such a compassionate, understanding and supportive fashion. Her book is written from the rare perspective of someone who actually knows first-hand the confusion, fear and frustrations of a panic sufferer. This book should be a must read for anyone who is trying to find their way in that frightening world. For those in the role of a support person, this book is a fast and easy way to gain a greater sensitivity of a panic and anxiety sufferer's experiences as well as education on how to offer more effective support."*

**Sandy Vilas, MCC**
CEO, Coach U, a worldwide coach training school

*"This set of instructions has helped me greatly."*

**K.P.C.** from San Diego, CA

*"I have so enjoyed and appreciated your book, Linda. It is so interesting and informative and full of hope and encouragement. I liked the calming effect it had on me as I read, and realised the techniques are good for the general population, as well as being very educational and insightful about panic and anxiety disorder."*

**Rhonda Schier** from Rapid City, SD

*"When I first picked up 'Panic and Anxiety Disorder: 121 Tips, Real-life Advice, Resources & More,' I was drawn to its calm, down-to-earth approach to self-help. Linda's tips, while pinpointing individual aspects of anxiety, actually address the very simple, basic, moment-by-moment steps to follow in order to successfully survive just about any stressful inner conflict. Her guidance is straightforward and simultaneously profound. Linda Manassee Buell has written this book with the compassion and personal landscape of someone who lived in the cave of fear, and who's triumphantly emerged into the sunshine."*

**Diane Duncan** from Pioneer, CA

*"Linda's book gave me greater empathy for the day-to-day struggles and concerns of people diagnosed with panic disorder."*

**Barbara Green** from Denver, CO

*"This book is a valuable addition to the others on the subject. Written in a direct and compassionate voice, it provides great insight and assistance to anyone connected to this disorder. I myself do not suffer from it; however, I'm close to a number of people who do. This book is a tremendous help to those of us who must learn to cope with a loved one who has a panic/anxiety disorder. And it provides an excellent tool to*

*begin safely discussing the topic with that loved one. Lastly, I've had the privilege to meet the author on a couple of occasions and talk about the issue—she is truly knowledgeable, sensitive, and passionate about it."*

**Andrew Chapman**
Speaker and author of
*Self-Publishing for Successful Fundraising*

*"We've been able to pass copies of your book on to a couple of friends who have some type of panic disorder and they have really appreciated it. It is helpful information for their families and 'support people' too. We were interested to read the book just to learn more. Now that we gave both of our books away, I had to order another copy for our home library. It really is a helpful reference! Thanks."*

**Donna Petersen** from Stockton, CA

# Overcome Panic and Anxiety Disorder

## 121 Tips, Real-life Advice, Resources & More

Linda Manassee Buell

CAPSTONE

This edition published by
Capstone Publishing Ltd. (a Wiley Company)
The Atrium, Southern Gate, Chichester, PO19 8SQ, UK.
www.wileyeurope.com

Email (for orders and customer service enquiries): cs-books@wiley.co.uk

*Other Wiley Editorial Offices*

Wiley-VCH Verlag GmbH, Boschstr. 12, D-69469 Weinheim, Germany
John Wiley & Sons Australia Ltd, 42 McDougall Street, Milton, Queensland 4064, Australia
John Wiley & Sons (Asia) Pte Ltd, 2 Clementi Loop #02-01, Jin Xing Distripark, Singapore 129809

Wiley also publishes its books in a variety of electronic formats. Some content that appears in print may not be available in electronic books.

A catalogue record for this book is available from the British Library.

ISBN 13: 978-1-90646-532-2

Typeset by SNP Best-set Typesetter Ltd., Hong Kong

Substantial discounts on bulk quantities of Capstone Books are available to corporations, professional associations and other organisations. For details telephone John Wiley & Sons on (+44) 1243-770441, fax (+44) 1243 770571 or email corporatedevelopment@wiley.co.uk

# Contents

# Foreword

I am delighted and honoured to be invited to write the Foreword to this excellent book. For the past 30 years I've been carrying out research to increase understanding and refine the available treatments for anxiety and depression. If anyone in 1980 had suggested when I qualified as a Clinical Psychologist that the day would come when I would find it necessary to employ anything other than pure psychological therapy to deal with difficulties within my own life, I would have hotly refuted this as being as improbable as dying in a plane crash—possible, yes, but only infinitesimally so. But at a particular period in my life, a number of powerful events occurred simultaneously, which tested my coping skills to the limit—and then beyond.

My very being protested that there was no way I would ever agree to seek additional assistance from anything or anyone outside of my field of expertise of Cognitive Behavioural Psychotherapy. Yet when close family pointed out that I must be unaware of how much I had over-reacted to an event, and cited the disproportionate fury of my response, I then felt completely overwhelmed. I admit that my position was worse than this; I *did* fully realise at the time what I was doing, but I was unable to react in any other way. Clearly being an expert may protect, but can't guarantee staying on track.

At this point I explored further options for myself, in addition to the cognitive behavioural techniques. The combinations that I employed made a significant difference to my distress, to my enormous relief! The level of misery I had been experiencing was unprecedented, and the inordinate effort it took to accept further help was in direct proportion to this. Having 'come out of the closet' regarding accessing a range of therapy tools in my time of need—I find that my disclosure is responded to with both respect, support. . . . and reciprocal revelations.

Linda's personal message makes the book approachable, appealing, and highly readable. Reading through the 121 tips, I was forcibly struck with how Linda has clearly followed her own advice from tip one onward—to become as well informed as possible. She clearly walks her talk. The finished book is small and light, but is a real heavyweight in that it is packed with useful and effective suggestions. It would be impossible to have this level of concise information, alongside indepth instruction on how to carry out all the advice. So, tip by tip, I found myself employing so many of the very techniques that I have researched and written about. And as I put the tips into practice, I really began to notice a perceptible lift in my mood.

When you go through the 121 Tips, chances are you will recognise and actually know very well *how* they should be implemented—you just need reminding to do them NOW! This book does not go into great 'how to' detail, but if you really do follow tip one, in your reading, you're bound to come across more detailed 'how to do it' instruction. So for example, Linda gives one paragraph with a succinct tip about breathing, rather than providing five pages of detailed relaxation exercises. So I believe that this brevity—one paragraph vs. 5 pages—is definitely a strength of Linda's book. It keeps the book portable and ensures it is user friendly, and even discreet.

In conclusion, I can really highly recommend this book. Given its compact format, you will probably be able to comfortably read it all the way through. Why not also treat it as a 'lucky dip', which you open at random, and then follow through the Tips on that page? If you are unclear about 'how'—go back to Tip one—which I am sure you now remember!

From my personal experience, you really can reclaim your life!

Elaine Iljon Foreman, Chartered Clinical Psychologist, director of Freedom to Fly and co-author of *Overcoming Anxiety For Dummies*

Elaine Iljon Foreman is a Chartered Clinical Psychologist and Associate Fellow of the British Psychological Society. Elaine specialises in the treatment of fear of flying as well as other anxiety related problems, including panic attacks, claustrophobia, agoraphobia, post-traumatic stress disorder and specific phobias. She is a Consultant Specialist in Cognitive Behaviour Therapy, accredited with the British Association for Behavioural and Cognitive Psychotherapy, and a Fellow of the Institute of Travel and Tourism. In addition, Elaine is Chair of the Ethics Committee of the United Kingdom Council For Psychotherapy.

Elaine's highly specialised Freedom to Fly™ Treatment Programme for the fear of flying, and the Freedom from Fear approach for other anxiety-based problems have been developed utilising her thirty years of clinical experience and ongoing research and development of cognitive behaviour therapy.

She started research into the treatment of anxiety in 1976 at the Middlesex Hospital Medical School and her continuing interest and success have brought invitations to present her findings in Europe, the Americas, Australia and the Far East. In addition she co-ordinates international research into the field of treatment for fear of flying. Her presentations and workshops are given both nationally and internationally on an ongoing basis to professional and self-help audiences.

Elaine's professional views are regularly sought by TV and radio in recognition of her innovative clinical research into anxieties and phobias, international conference presentations, workshops, and published material in her specialist field. Her most recent publications are *Overcoming Anxiety For Dummies* and *Overcoming Depression For Dummies*, co-authored with Charles Elliott and Laura Smith. In addition she has co-authored

*Fly Away Fear, A Self-Help Guide to Overcoming Fear of Flying* along with Lucas Van Gerwen, published by Karnac in May 2008.

Further information on the Freedom to Fly™ organisation can be found by visiting www.freedomtofly.biz. The Service Brochure detailing the range of services including workshops and psychological therapy can be obtained by emailing elaine@freedomtofly.biz

# Introduction

'Hi, my name is Linda Manassee Buell, and I have panic disorder with agoraphobia.' I remember saying those words out loud for the first time in 1994 at an anxiety clinic group session. I don't know if the tears that welled up in my eyes then were from my relief in finally knowing there was a name for what I had, or a new despair from knowing that I actually had this demanding, debilitating mystery illness. And today, I don't know if it's happiness or sadness that brings tears to my eyes. I do know that now there is hope.

My first major panic attack occurred during the summer of 1992 while I was on an airplane flight to Los Angeles, California, where I was scheduled to attend a major business meeting. After that first frightening attack and numerous additional 'aftershock' attacks, I spent the following year and a half looking for an answer to what was wrong with me. I started with a troop of medical doctors, three trips to the hospital, and finally a therapist when the doctors told me they couldn't find anything wrong. I worked with the therapist for over a year before I was told that I had Panic Disorder with Agoraphobia. Fast-forward to today. It's now three cities and five therapists later and what feels like a million miles further on my quest for answers. I have learned how to rid myself of agoraphobia and live with panic disorder.

I've felt so much, both physically and emotionally, on this journey and I believe what I have discovered might be of help to you or yours.

It's important for you to know that I am not a therapist. I am just one of the many millions of people who have this disorder. It's estimated that 23 million people suffer with anxiety disorders in America alone. Studies have also shown similar 'panic attack' symptoms can be found in people in other countries around the world.

Change for any one of us starts with each of us individually. When we become educated about our disorder, we can then share and educate others. When we embrace and accept this disorder, then hopefully our friends and families will become more understanding about what it is really about. When we decide to take steps to help ourselves live with this disorder, then others can take steps to better help us live with it. When we decide that there isn't a stigma attached to this disorder, then perhaps others can let go of their preconceptions about it.

I admit that over the years I have searched for a magic pill, hoping to find one that would just make this thing go away. However, I have now come to see this disorder as an 'energy' disorder, wherein the 'out of control' panic energy is actually part of the same energy that was in my body before the first panic attack. This perspective allows me to have the ability and tools to redirect this into healthy and productive energy. One of my decisions has been to direct this energy into helping myself and others.

I have written this book because I get angry at how misunderstood this disorder has been by those of us with it, and certainly by those without.

I get frustrated at the remarkable lack of information easily available to us.

I get a feeling of despair when the only qualified professional is miles or cities away, and there is no way to get there for help.

I'm tired of friends and family members thinking I can cure this condition simply by 'bucking up.'

I am saddened when I think of all the people who are trying to live with panic disorder (both those who know of their diagnosis and those who do not yet know) and who are desperately trying to hide or mask their situation.

If you have any kind of anxiety disorder, with or without a phobia, please know you are not alone, you aren't broken, and you don't need to be fixed. I'd like you to know that you are a beautiful and wonderful human being, and you can still live a magnificent life right now, today and every day. If you don't suffer from any kind of disorder or phobia and you're still reading this book, thank you for taking the time to educate yourself and for caring about those who do suffer.

With love,
Linda

*No one can understand the true nature of your inner world. It can be a lonely feeling. And this is true for all, no matter what is going on for them in their lives. So I guess in that, we are really not alone after all.*

Linda Manassee Buell

# You're Not Alone

A panic attack or one of the anxiety disorders can happen to anyone; they are not selective disorders. Some of the celebrities below have experienced panic attacks, others know what it feels like to have social phobia, and some have even been agoraphobic. You're in good company:

- *Aretha Franklin,* singer
- *Nicholas Cage,* actor
- *Michael Jackson,* singer
- *Johnny Depp,* actor
- *Alanis Morissette,* singer
- *Burt Reynolds,* actor
- *Kim Basinger,* actress
- *Oprah Winfrey,* host
- *Barbra Streisand,* singer
- *Courtney Love,* singer
- *Naomi Campbell,* model
- *David Bowie,* singer
- *Charlotte Brontë,* author
- *Sigmund Freud,* psychiatrist
- *Sir Isaac Newton,* scientist
- *Abraham Lincoln,* president

Source: *The Anxiety Panic Internet Resource* (www.algy.com/anxiety)

[About six weeks after my first panic attack—before I knew they were panic attacks.]

*Whatever you are, you've been in my life long enough now. I accept you are here for a reason. I am looking for answers. I've had a million thoughts while you've been here and I've also hidden a million thoughts. Am I looking too hard for the answer? . . . I hate this! I hate this feeling! I hate being sick! I'm not who I thought I was, I'm not the strong sufferer in silence, the stoic person. I feel helpless. Is it OK to feel helpless? I want to be perfect. . . . I will try to give this time. I will try to observe and be with the feelings.*

Journal entry, August 30, 1992
Linda Manassee Buell

# 1 Seek Professional Help

*"I was uneducated about what I had. I was embarrassed at first and mad about my condition. I kept thinking, 'Why has this got to hit me, of all people?' I've always thought of myself as a laid-back guy."*

Football Hall of Famer Earl Campbell
"America Undercover," HBO, September 16, 1999

*"Trust your instincts in seeking help. Do not give up the search for effective, proven treatments—is possibly the most important advice you can get from this author who has been there and who cares and is mindful about her readers."*

Emanuel Maidenberg, Ph.D.
Assistant Clinical Professor of Psychiatry, UCLA

My personal experience with Panic and Anxiety Disorder has been shared with six psychologists, four medical doctors, three chiropractors, three holistic health practitioners (massage therapists) and a variety of other medical professionals. And I felt that a lot of them didn't really 'listen' to me. Maybe that's why it took 18 months before I finally received a correct diagnosis for what was causing my suffering.

Ever since my first panic attack, even when my 'gut' reaction told me these doctors' medical advice wasn't being helpful, I continued seeing them for way too long and paying way too much money. Like many people, I suppose, I assumed that a professional knows more than I do, so I just hung in there indefinitely in unsatisfactory situations.

As time went by, I discovered they didn't always know more about my particular situation than I did, or they just didn't want to take the time to know me and what I was experiencing. It seemed to me it was easier or more convenient for them to find a category for me and give me some standard answer that had served them in the past for what they perceived to be a similar situation.

Despite all those not-so-good experiences, however, I still recommend getting professional help. Fortunately, I've found there are some very knowledgeable people available. I just needed to do some focused research to find them, seek advice from others experiencing what I was experiencing and really take the time to talk and ask questions of medical professionals before I committed my time and resources to them. In this process, one truly important value I found is to give yourself permission to change professionals if the relationship shifts, changes or doesn't feel right.

You might even want to have a team made up of different medical professionals supporting you to call on when needed. My team includes a medical doctor who makes sure my physical body is in good shape; a psychologist to help me with my desensitisation issues; a chiropractor using Applied Kinesiology, along with a Holistic Health Practitioner for massage and cranial sacral therapy, who help keep my body's energy flow positive; and a coach who helps me see life's beautiful forest through the trees.

# 1

Become as well-informed as possible. Today there are many treatment approaches and combinations of approaches available to you.

# 2

Visit your library or look on the Internet for information about successful therapies. Remember to check the authors of all information to ensure that they are reliable sources.

# 3

Seek diagnoses from a mental health professional. Don't rely on self-diagnosis or on your belief of what you 'think may be the problem.'

# 4

Find trained professionals in your area by contacting organisations such as the Anxiety Disorders Association of America, the American Psychiatric Association, the American Psychological Association, or the Association for Advancement of Behavior Therapy. These organisations also offer online resources and referral information.

# 5

Be aware that many therapists work in multiple areas. Look for a professional who specialises in anxiety and panic disorders.

# 6

Ask about cognitive-behavioural therapy. Experience has shown this type of therapy to be one of the most effective and long-lasting treatments available for people with panic disorder.

# 7

Keep in mind that any decision regarding taking medication is highly personal. It should only be made in conjunction with your mental health professional.

# 8

Seek the advice of a psychopharmacologist (a physician trained to prescribe different types of medications) regarding appropriate medication available for panic disorder.

# 9

Ask about the types of medications available, their effectiveness, dosages and side effects so that you have a good understanding of what to expect. Additional information can be found in your library and on the Internet.

# 10

Learn about medical conditions that mimic anxiety symptoms. Don't automatically assume you have any of these conditions without asking your physician to perform the appropriate medical tests.

# 11

Get a complete physical, including a check of your thyroid, blood iron levels and vestibular system. This can be a big help in ruling out some of your biggest fears. Once you've had your physical, remind yourself that you are healthy.

# 12

Don't hesitate to find another doctor if you feel your current doctor doesn't understand your specific needs or is uneducated about panic disorder. Don't let him or her intimidate you or discount how you're feeling.

# 13

Know that there are legal rights in the workplace to which you are entitled if you need protection.

*What is going on? I feel anxious. I'm going to see a new doctor.* [My therapist of the last year just told me that I have Panic Disorder with Agoraphobia.]

*Labelling what I have makes something real that I never acknowledged before. I don't want it to have a name. When I was sick before, I wanted to know what it was—now I don't. If I say I have something—then it will get worse. I want to fight it, not acknowledge it, give it attention. I want to put it away.*

*I want this to go away. I want to function in life again. What's worse? To live a lie with hidden feelings or to feel like this?*

Journal entry, February 9, 1994
Linda Manassee Buell

# 2 Your Mind and Body Are Connected

*"I still don't know what causes panic disorder. Nobody does exactly. But over time I have discovered this much about myself: if I work for about 10 days straight and don't rest like I should, I'm asking for trouble. That's when I'm most likely to be hit with a panic attack."*

Football Hall of Famer Earl Campbell
"Rush of Fear," People Magazine, November 4, 1991

*"Become friends with your body sensations so your mind will learn that they are not dangerous. It is a difficult endeavour since your brain has associated them with danger. But it is a significant key to success."*

Stéphane Bouchard, Ph.D.
University of Quebec (Canada)
Department of Psychoeducation and Psychology

My panic attacks and anticipatory anxiety create a number of immediate physical changes in my body. These sensations are triggered from my sudden and unexpected fearful thoughts and can include nausea, headaches and chest pains, among other symptoms. It might also work in the reverse order: where a preceding physical feeling can trigger worry or fearful thoughts that then lead to an attack. For instance, I might wake up feeling a bit of nausea, which then gets my mind thinking, which leads to worry about the nausea and fear of what terrible thing it might mean. I can experience this chain of events, all the while being aware that this could lead to my experiencing a panic attack which unto itself can create more worry and fear.

Sleep, exercise, diet and stress all affect the way we feel and therefore think. Each one of us is a fully integrated being although most of the time we don't use the power of that integration. If I can have thoughts that trigger unpleasant sensations in my body, then conversely, I can also have thoughts that trigger pleasant sensations. With that in mind, I can regulate my internal world with good and consistent sleep patterns, regular exercise, healthy eating and pre-managing in order to create low-stress or stress-free situations. I should then be able to create a balanced connection for my body and mind.

When we feel good and have good energy, then we have good internal reserves to deal with whatever shows up. I know that I must be very disciplined with myself in order to keep my reserves high at all times. To that end, I take control and plan my daily activities for the good of both my body and my mind.

# 14

Take charge of your life. Become an expert on you.

# 15

Don't skip meals, especially breakfast. Make sure you eat three healthy meals each and every day.

# 16

Eliminate caffeine and other foods that tend to trigger chemical reactions of the nervous system. Remember that chocolate has caffeine, as do many foods that may surprise you. Get in the habit of reading food labels.

# 17

Keep a complete food journal and compare this with any increased anxiety. You may have food allergies and sensitivities that can trigger attacks.

# 18

Check with a nutritional specialist to find out if nutritional imbalances are influencing your panic disorder symptoms. Untreated hypoglycaemia can trigger panic attacks.

# 19

Always check with your doctor regarding all prescription drugs, including asthma medications and diet pills. Stimulants such as pseudoephedrine, found in many over-the-counter medications for colds, allergies and sinus problems, may induce panic attacks in some people. Make it your practice to read all medication labels.

# 20

Recognise hyperventilation, or rapid breathing, for what it is and all the physical symptoms it causes, such as dizziness, confusion, or numbness or tingling in your arms and legs. Hyperventilation is experienced by more than half of the people who have panic attacks, and isn't dangerous. There are a number of techniques you can use to calm your breathing.

# 21

Teach yourself about the parasympathetic and sympathetic nervous systems and their chemical reactions. Get to know the different ways adrenaline impacts your body.

# 22

Learn to relax when any symptoms caused by chemical reactions in your body trigger an anxiety or panic attack. They aren't harmful and they will dissipate.

# 23

Read books about other disorders with biochemical complications. There are a number of similarities that might be helpful to know about. By understanding more about what triggers your panic, you can learn how to change these conditions.

# 24

Be aware that the fluctuation of premenopause hormonal changes might make one especially symptomatic. Women should establish a logbook to find out if any of the panic disorder symptoms track to monthly menstrual cycles.

# 25

Identify your personal physical response to panic. Do your hands tingle? Does your chest hurt? Are you nauseous? By knowing how you physically respond, you no longer have to be afraid of the physical symptoms.

# 26

Know that your symptoms can vary over time. Very few people's symptoms are always the same. A difference or change in your panic symptoms or an increased intensity does not mean there is something else wrong with you or that you are in greater danger.

# 27

Realise that you very well could be overly vigilant about your body and excessively monitoring any and all changes. You may find that most of these are actually normal sensations or ones that you are producing by your fearful thoughts.

# 28

Get a good night's sleep. A lack of sleep can contribute to increased anxiety and panic.

*I'm so tired! And it just goes on and on. 5.30 AM wouldn't be so bad if I'd go to sleep early. The nice part was not getting up in the middle of the night, or is this the middle of the night? I notice I ask myself how I feel every morning. Wake up; look for the fear and panic. Am I having anticipatory anxiety? Meditate, everywhere I read it says meditate. This journalling is sort of my meditation. I was going to add just 10 minutes more a morning; that shouldn't be hard. But it has been. . . . Listen deeply to my soul. Look within. I never really stop thinking because I'm always then thinking about how I'm not thinking.*

Journal entry, September 6, 1995
Linda Manassee Buell

# 3 Breathing

*"If I could only do one thing in a session, I would always
work with the person's breathing. When breath is flowing
naturally, everything benefits: body, mind and spirit."*

Gay Hendricks, Ph.D.
Author of *Conscious Breathing* and
(with Dr. Kathlyn Hendricks) *Breathing Ecstasy*

The most important resource each of us has available to us every moment of every day is within us. It is our breathing. I have learned over the years, even relearned, the importance of knowing how to breathe correctly and beneficially.

It's interesting to me that we all knew how to breathe properly when we were born. As infants, we lay in our cribs and just did it. Correct breathing is a relaxed process that finds the stomach moving easily out and in, not expanding our chest as much as we can. Watch a baby sleep and you can see this easy, natural stomach motion. Then try to recall when you last saw an adult breathing with their stomach going out and in. That's because most of us were taught to "stand up straight and hold our stomachs in." And what's happened because of this? As we grew up, we learned how to breathe in our chests even as we naturally felt a physical resistance. Most people are in the unconscious habit of taking rapid and short chest breaths. Add to that some stress and anxiety, some dizziness and a few chest pains, and you've got many of the physical makings of an oncoming panic attack.

Think of your breath as being like a metronome keeping pace with the energy in your body. If you're breathing fast, then your internal rhythms are likewise moving rapidly. When you can slow your breath down, you can slow your inner world down. I actually wear clothes that fit more loosely around the waist so I can better check in with my breathing throughout the day. Healthy breathing is cleansing, clearing and calming, and it's a valuable resource we all carry with us wherever we go.

# 29

Avoid the kind of "shallow breathing" that is common among panic disorder sufferers. If you are underbreathing while you're in a calm state, imagine what happens when you are confronted with an anxiety-producing situation.

# 30

Know how to prevent hyperventilation or rapid breathing in order to bring about a balance in the oxygen-to-carbon dioxide ratio in your body. This can actually help reduce the physical symptoms of panic.

# 31

Breathe from your abdomen and through your nose. This is known as breathing diaphragmatically and can calm you, relax you and ground you.

# 32

Lie on your back and put a book on your stomach. Breathe in and let your stomach expand. Watch yourself to be sure the book rises up. As you exhale, watch the book sink back down.

# 33

Place your hands on your stomach when sitting or lying down and feel your stomach move in and out with healthy diaphragmatic breaths. Practise maintaining slow, smooth breathing.

# 34

Focus your concentration on expanding your stomach when inhaling and keeping your chest still. Then count slowly to slow down your exhalations. This focused concentration can also distract you from fearful, panic-type thoughts.

# 35

Try imagining yourself lying down on some cool grass with a light breeze gently blowing across your face, or sitting in the warm sand watching the beautiful blue of the ocean waves lapping gently on shore. Now check to see if you are breathing diaphragmatically.

## 36

Visualise a white cleansing light entering the bottom of your feet and travelling upward throughout your body as you breathe in. As you exhale, visualise the release of all the stress that the white light collected.

## 37

Imagine, while breathing in, that you are expanding the space within and throughout your body to make room for your panic energy. If there is too much energy to hold, release the excess with each outward breath.

## 38

Take a bit longer when exhaling versus inhaling. Exhaling triggers your parasympathetic nervous system, which is tied to your relaxation system.

## 39

Let go of the need to deliberately hold in your stomach or wear tight clothes. Having been taught to stand up straight and hold in your stomach quite probably has led to upper chest breathing, resulting in undefined chest pains or lightheadedness.

# 40

Practise diaphragmatic breathing every time you feel any anxiety or panic. Keep bringing your attention back to your breathing, feeling your stomach move slowly in and out.

# 41

Keep practising, and then practise some more. Once the technique is mastered, diaphragmatic breathing can be done anywhere and at any time. Notice your breathing several times throughout the day.

# 42

Begin breathing diaphragmatically as soon as you recognise a panic-type thought or physical sensation. This will help you stop the sequence of events that leads to a panic attack.

# 43

Place little red stickers or something similar around your home and work environment. Take a one- to two-minute breathing break each time you see one.

*Humour—that's a great sign. I get so inside myself with doom and gloom I'm glad to see that I can laugh at myself. Everything can't be that bad when you can still laugh at yourself! The pain is in my physical body—not my spiritual body. The pain is in my past, in my memories. My mind filters through the demons of the past. I want to fill the vase with love. I love and appreciate myself just the way I am. I say this into the mirror, into the soul.*

Journal entry, July 25, 1996
Linda Manassee Buell

# 4 Centre Yourself

*"You have to organise your mind and don't let it fly off the handle."*

Singer, songwriter, and actor Donny Osmond
"48 Hours," CBS Worldwide, August 10, 2000

*"What does it mean to be centred? Some define it by being always calm and comfortable no matter what is transpiring. A more powerful definition is to give your centre over to what you are doing, so that there is no room for worry or unnecessary reactions. Yet the most profound definition of centring of all is to give your centre away to the moment at hand. Without holding onto any image of one's self, without clutching to fears of that self becoming harmed, there is no 'self' to become flustered or distressed. To accomplish this, one must only be willing to accept one's death without fear. Only then can one truly forget oneself and allow one's world to come more fully alive. Only without fear of dying can one be in the world as if it is the most wonderful moment that exists."*

Jim Spira, Ph.D., M.P.H., ABPP
Director, Institute For Health Psychology,
Solana Beach, CA

My personal coach is a wonderful woman who can sense and will tell me when I'm 'in my body' or 'out of my body.' She usually makes these comments when I'm revved up explaining events after a panic attack, or when I'm feeling anxious about something.

What she means is I'm not breathing diaphragmatically (from my abdomen) or even noticing how I'm breathing. My mind chatter is very active and I'm not paying attention to anything specific in the moment. I'm too busy thinking about the future or the past. I can feel surges of energy in my body and might even feel edgy. There are also times when I bang into things or trip while walking. My body is basically on its own, seemingly out of control. She's helped me to recognise in myself when this is happening and taught me how to bring myself back to centre.

This is when I can truly find that the main benefit of being centred is the calm within and around me. Even if something outside of me is in chaos, I'm not. I approach my day and my life like the line from the Eagles' song, 'with a peaceful, easy feeling.' If you're doing desensitisation work and the anxiety is starting to rise, by being centred you can return to your body, calm your system and support your success. If, on a daily basis, you practise being centred while you're feeling fine, your recovery from a panic attack can be quicker. Your body will know where to go by previous training and experience. Make it a habit to live from a centred place, you'll love how you feel.

# 44

Think of panic as nothing more than an excess of high energy in your body. You have the power to convert this energy and use it in a way that will serve your needs. This is probably the same high energy that has helped you succeed at other things in your past.

# 45

Learn how to relax your body and release all the tension and strain it experiences when dealing with panic symptoms. Go limp like a rag doll; shake your arms; wiggle your legs.

# 46

Tense and relax specific muscles in various parts of your body. Notice how you cannot be tense and relaxed at the same time.

# 47

Learn about biofeedback, which can teach you to consciously regulate a number of your own autonomic functions, like heart rate and blood pressure. This combines a variety of relaxation methods using instruments that monitor your individual responses.

# 48

Utilise meditation, a mantra (a calming word or phrase you repeat) and diaphragmatic breathing when negative thoughts appear. Getting centred and grounding yourself can calm your mind and physical symptoms and help you stay focused on the present.

# 49

Repeat a mantra to steady and quiet the mind at any time and in any place. Your mantra can also be used as an excellent preparation for a good night's sleep.

# 50

Enjoy regular massage therapy to help you relax, slow your heart rate and breathe more deeply. Massage grounds you and puts you in touch with your body.

# 51

Experience cranial sacral therapy, acupuncture, Reiki and applied kinesiology. All of these modalities are designed to unblock your body's energy and help it flow.

# 52

Start a journal and write down your feelings and your emotions. Journal writing is a safe way to stay in touch with how you feel and what you think in all aspects of your life.

# 53

Become an expert at recognising your own automatic negative thoughts. Break down each anxious thought until it is very specific. The less vague your thoughts are, the easier it is to refute them and reduce your anxiety.

# 54

Revise these unhelpful thoughts into positive, supportive thoughts. Find something positive to say, then both say and write it.

# 55

Develop personal affirmations or positive statements about the progress you're making, no matter how great or how small. These can be related to your panic disorder or may also be about life in general.

# 56

Challenge your automatic negative thoughts consistently. You'll probably have to apply your new alternative thoughts many, many times before they can automatically replace the old thoughts. Know that's just part of the process.

# 57

Make it a goal to continually learn and use new positive thoughts. The automatic negative thoughts were once learned and can be unlearned and replaced.

# 58

Replace your statements that begin with 'What if . . .' with 'This is how I'll handle . . .'. This helps in generating new coping thoughts rather than replaying old fearful thoughts.

# 59

Don't argue with yourself. When your inner voices get going, don't encourage them by engaging in arguments with them.

# 60

Say 'Stop!' when an old negative thought appears. Tell yourself you are no longer buying into any negative thoughts.

# 61

Use your suffering as a teacher. See your attachments and fears as the first step in helping you set yourself free.

# 62

Become a personal observer, as if you were outside your panic looking in. Shifting your perspective can take the suffering away.

# 63

Ask yourself, 'What parts of me are not feeling fear?' Some part of you is probably not feeling afraid.

*Sitting in the darkness*
*Feeling all alone*
*Knowing that I'm scared to death*
*Braving life alone*

*No one's there to guide me*
*I'm trying to find my way*
*But demons in the darkness*
*Keep scaring me away*

*I hum the songs of comfort*
*I search into my heart*
*I know that I'm being guided*
*Something else is playing a part*

*A ray of light is shining*
*And now it's all around*
*The beauty's unbelievable*
*And comfort's finally found*

*The light is there to guide me*
*It's there to see me through*
*Just turn inside to see it*
*It's always there for you*

Journal entry, February 7, 1997
(An update from January 30, 1996)
Linda Manassee Buell

# 5 Systematic Desensitisation

*"There are times when I remember if I had the choice of walking on stage or dying—I would have chosen death. It's that scary."*

Singer, songwriter, and actor Donny Osmond
"48 Hours," CBS Worldwide, August 10, 2000

*"Nothing works better toward overcoming a fear than facing it—especially when this is done systematically and in small increments. Furthermore, improvement resulting from desensitisation does not disappear weeks or months later. Once you've fully densensitised yourself to a phobic situation in real life, you can remain free of fear."*

Edmond J. Bourne, Ph.D.
author of *The Anxiety and Phobia Workbook*,
Third Edition

I once tried a process called 'flooding' before a trip I had to make. The process is probably best explained by one therapist's comment to me, 'I don't care if you have to crawl to get there, you're going.' It's a little like 'face the fear and do it anyway,' only in my case, it was 'face the fear and have a panic attack.' Before travelling, I would become physically sick for two to three days just from the anticipatory anxiety. Sometimes I made the trip, and sometimes I didn't.

I did a lot of flooding for the first seven years of my panic disorder. Then the agoraphobia got worse and I would flood just to go to a movie, a restaurant or across town, even if my closest support person, my husband, was with me. It wasn't fun and it didn't help me. I wasn't able to repeat activities with less anxiety afterwards, which was the goal. I was, in my opinion, teaching myself just how to do things and feel lousy. Once I figured that out, I looked for another method—one where I could teach myself how to do things and feel great. I wanted to set up new conditions around these old experiences.

Using systematic desensitisation, I was able to help my body begin to understand at a visceral, instinctive, level that doing things could be a pleasant experience. Now I don't force things anymore and I am much more likely to be successful with them. I can now travel anywhere in the greater San Diego area—even on the expressways in traffic—versus my original limitation of a five-mile radius from my house using only lightly travelled side streets. I can once again go to movies, the theatre, conferences and seminars. I even took my nieces to a water park on the far side of town this past summer.

I hadn't realised how small and seemingly comfortable I had made my little world until I started adding back to make it larger again. I didn't realise how many times I had made excuses for not attending dinner engagements, parties and other social events. I even created a home-based business so I didn't have to leave my house at all. Now I can consciously and willingly choose when I want to leave my house, and it feels great.

# 64

Don't surrender to the fear, as that will allow it to grow and become more powerful. The more you practise avoidance, the harder it becomes to treat your anxiety and panic.

# 65

Don't avoid situations or places for fear of having a panic attack. This is called agoraphobia, and it creates a false illusion of safety. It can actually cause the fear to grow in anticipation.

# 66

Make a conscious and determined effort to teach yourself to stop avoiding situations and places. You taught yourself to avoid these things in the first place; you can teach yourself to stop.

# 67

Practise going places and putting yourself into situations you would normally avoid. This desensitisation process works best in the long run when you break it down into small steps.

# 68

Give yourself permission to make the steps as small as you need when you begin. The key is to take a step no matter how small, and to take it slowly yet surely.

# 69

Stay with it. When you feel anxious, go at least the same distance as you went previously. By not going out, you again set yourself up for continued avoidance.

# 70

Repeat, repeat and repeat your practice. The goal is to move from doing things with apprehension to doing them with confidence. Repeat an activity until you feel confident.

# 71

Don't try to move too fast. It can keep you from feeling confident. It isn't about playing 'tag' with your destination and then running home, or tolerating high levels of anxiety; it's about learning to enjoy being wherever you want to go.

# 72

Be willing to put up with some temporary minor discomforts. These uncomfortable sensations are not life-threatening.

# 73

Continue to plot out new destinations or events and stick to a desensitisation schedule. Do this until you can move about so freely that you become bored with the entire process.

# 74

Stop the comments from the judgmental part of yourself Practising going places and into situations does take a lot of time and energy. That's okay.

# 75

Write down your negative thoughts as you do your desensitisation work so that you can refute them and replace them. You can always find alternative thoughts to replace negative ones.

# 76

Jot down lots of positive affirmations. Memorise and use these phrases throughout the day, wherever you go.

# 77

Get in the habit of using positive self-talk when you practise and even when you don't. If you use positive self-talk daily, it will be there automatically for you in times of high anxiety or panic.

# 78

Replace your negative thoughts with positive affirmations to help keep your thoughts of fear from spiralling, which just creates more fear and, therefore, more of the physical feelings of panic. Don't give the fear more power by focusing your thoughts in this area.

# 79

Look at setbacks as an opportunity for additional growth. Remember, a setback can only occur when you have had some success.

# 80

Shift from focusing on the anxiety to focusing on your destination. Visualise yourself at your location, smiling and enjoying yourself and your success.

# 81

Use the security of a cellular phone. You will always feel as if help is just a quick phone call away.

# 82

Remember to celebrate each success no matter how small. Cheer yourself, let yourself be happy and excited and then share it with others.

*I lost a part of me. It seems like it was the part that used to throw caution to the wind. I would say, "what the heck," and I never hesitated to go somewhere, expecting nothing much. What part of me does Chuck miss? I know—the carefree, laughing person sailing in the Caribbean. I don't laugh as much. I've become much more serious with life.*

Journal entry, October 7, 1999
Linda Manassee Buell

# 6 Distraction Techniques

*"You feel like you're having a hallucination,
that you're losing your mind."*

Singer/songwriter Naomi Judd
"Weekend Edition" Extra, June 6–7, 2001

*"Distraction Techniques help us in being freer; they distance us from
the problem. They have the power to place the panic attack in its right
measure. In fact, what we think is a lion; it is nothing more than a
shadow. A shadow that does not have to scare us. Whenever possible,
use Distraction Techniques coloured by sense of humour. Let go and
enjoy them. You will find that the lion does not attack you."*

Cristina Botella, Ph.D.
Professor of Psychology, Jaume I University (Spain)

O K, the truth is, there are just some times I can't get my
rapid-fire mind chatter to stop. I pull out all my breathing
and centring techniques but if I'm overtired or out of
energy, I just can't focus. So I go to my tool called 'distraction
techniques.' These are things that can take my mind off myself
and on to something else. I've found that a specific technique,

like reading, works fine in one moment, but might not work the next. Early on, I was using distraction techniques more often than breathing and centring because I wasn't very good at those yet. I hadn't had enough practice to be able to go easily and quickly to a diaphragmatic breath. It wasn't yet ingrained as a habit.

In my early years of having panic disorder, I would actually keep a written list of possible distractions I might be able to utilise. It included letters that needed writing, reading material, Internet research, movies or television selections on tape, walking, swimming and others. For times when my mind was racing or I was feeling anxious, even panicky, I could look at my list and find a thing or things that I thought would be helpful in that moment.

Today I don't need to make a list, but that doesn't mean I don't use distraction techniques—I do. I use them when I feel they can be of additional help or when the situation is not conducive to breathing and centring. And I use only those that are enjoyable. (Perhaps while stopped at a traffic light, you've looked over at the woman in the car next to you who's singing quite boisterously along with her favorite tunes all by herself. Hi! That could be me!)

# 83

Use distraction to change your thoughts of desperation to thoughts of relaxation. Remember, the more desperate one is to relax, the more difficult relaxation can be.

# 84

Lie on the ground and visualise your anxiety as energy that is draining into the core of the earth. Ask the universe to disperse it for you.

# 85

Dig in the earth or just feel the soil. Gardening can be a great way for you to become grounded and centred.

# 86

Get a child's bucket and shovel set and head for the nearest playground sandbox or a beach. Dig a hole, rearrange the sand, or build a sandcastle.

# 87

Use humour whenever you can. Laughing is a great way to release stress.

# 88

Engage in conversation as a method to decrease stress and anxiety, but concentrate on really listening to the other person rather than trying to carry or monopolise the conversation.

# 89

Find helpful techniques to stop negative talk when it begins. Snapping a rubber band around your wrist can serve as a reminder to return to the present moment.

# 90

Count objects around you or count backward from 1000 by 3's or 7's. This will help bring your attention back to the present moment and away from future fearful thoughts.

# 91

Walk slowly while first allowing your heel to touch the ground, then your toes. Feel each part of your foot touch the ground. Feel your feet firmly on the ground.

# 92

Exercise regularly with a programme that works for you. There are many types to choose from, but remember that every person's body reacts differently to different types of exercise. Avoid any that can actually increase your panic symptoms.

# 93

Be aware that exercising your muscles produces lactic acid, which can also increase your anxiety. Therefore, be gradual in your exercise approach.

# 94

Consider getting a dog or cat. Animals can be very therapeutic and give unconditional love.

*I'm sitting on a wooden park bench looking out over the vast blue ocean! I feel such joy as a cool breeze and gentle warmth from the sun caress my face. What a beautiful reward this moment is for me. It is perfect weather on a perfect day, and tears begin to spill from my eyes. I have finally made it from my home to this place for the first time by myself.*

*I have finally reached another plateau, step-by-step, day-by-day. While today's journey began just 30 miles ago, this accomplishment began years ago. My tears remind me how far I've actually come, even if my brain won't yet let me fully appreciate this wonderful event in my life. So I tell my brain to just be quiet, and I allow my heart to enjoy the sea and the sun. Other people sit nearby. They have no idea of the joy this journey has brought to me, nor I of their journey or joy. Yet we all share this same moment in time, in our own ways, together.*

Journal entry, June 5, 2000
Linda Manassee Buell

# 7 Accept Yourself

*"I'm here to say that it's real, it is very serious,
but it's treatable, and there is always hope and
I'm living proof because I don't have it anymore."*

Singer/songwriter Naomi Judd
"Weekend Edition" Extra, June 6–7, 2001

*"I don't think you're ever cured. I think it's something you
learn to deal with, you learn to handle."*

Singer, songwriter, and actor Donny Osmond
"48 Hours," CBS Worldwide, August 10, 2000

*"I don't say I'm over it. I've gotten educated.
If it happens, I know what to do."*

Football Hall of Famer Earl Campbell
"Former Grid Star Learns to Cope" by Jane Ciahattari,
Parade Magazine, September 5, 1999

*"In many situations change requires a prior step: accepting the distinction between an assumption and a perception. Until we recognize it, assumptions are our world; they seem like perceptions and are outside. Accepting that our fears are just within us, is the first step for a better life."*

Giuseppe Riva, Ph.D.
Senior Researcher, Applied Technology for Neuro-Psychology (Italy) Research Professor of General Psychology, Catholic University of Milan, Italy

The therapist told me I had Panic Disorder with Agoraphobia. And what I heard loud and clear was, 'You have a mental disorder.' As much as I want to tell you that it didn't bother me, it did, on a number of levels. Particularly the perfectionist in me who immediately became the unhappiest person I knew!!

For years, I told only a very select few about my diagnosis. Although my husband knew, I hid my disorder from my peers, my employees and even from other members of my family. When I couldn't travel or go somewhere, whether it was family or business related, I said it was because 'I had the flu.' I had the flu a lot in those early years of my panic disorder. After time, that led to changing my excuse to telling people I had a 'fear of flying.' Whatever I came up with, I felt friends and family should just understand I wasn't going to be there, that I shouldn't have to do anything to educate them further or tell them how I was really feeling.

At work, when travel got even more impossible for me, I sought out and got protection under the Americans With Disabilities Act, which effectively limited my travel for business. Within the corporate environment, however, people didn't understand why I was being given 'special treatment.' Now looking back on those years in the business world, I realise that it's no wonder they didn't understand. I wasn't being forthcoming; I wasn't being truthful; and I was secretly receiving special hidden arrangements from my boss and our company's human resources department not to have to attend all the company meetings I normally would.

If I wasn't going to be totally open and honest, how should I have expected anyone to understand? If I wasn't going to completely accept this disorder without any stigma attached, why should I have expected others to accept it? I had to start the work of letting go of my stigma and truly accepting that I had panic disorder. So I began to do just that. Does that mean those others now understand? For some people, yes, for others, more than they did before, and for still others, they might never understand. But it really doesn't matter to me anymore, because I know I've done everything I can to accept myself for who I am. And in the end, that's all that really matters.

# 95

Accept yourself as you are right now. How much shorter would your panic attack be if there were no negative judgments attached?

# 96

Know that you can't make yourself have a panic attack. Go ahead—try right now. Realise that you can't have one 'on demand,' and remember how much 'control' you have over your thinking when one arises the next time.

# 97

Understand that the mind and the body are connected. When the mind is disturbed, the body will follow. Put your mind into a comfortable state and the body will follow as well.

# 98

Treat yourself with lots of love. That's more important than getting over a panic attack, though it will actually help you do just that.

# 99

Don't confuse your 'panic' behaviours with your basic personality traits. Panic disorder causes symptoms which, in turn, determine behaviour. You are not your disease.

# 100

Stop labelling panic as 'bad.' Even in the worst situation, goodness can be found.

# 101

Don't get caught in other people's judgments of panic disorder and anxiety as a judgment on you. They don't know what they don't know.

# 102

Remember that your fight/flight response system can fire unexpectedly. Out-of-the-blue panic can occur again. Use this as an opportunity to double-check your mental and physical well-being.

# 103

Share your victories with your support community. Don't minimise your success—celebrate enthusiastically.

# 104

Don't think you have to learn how to live better with stress. Instead, learn how to create balance and calm in your life to minimise stress in the first place.

# 105

Learn how to say no to the things you really don't want in your life. You don't need or want panic disorder. Exercise your right to choose, and say no to panic anxiety.

# 106

Have compassion for all you have had to endure. There is a very strong person inside you who is helping you live with panic disorder.

# 107

Write down all of the wonderful things about yourself. Notice how anxiety disorder is not 'all' of you; it is just one aspect of your being.

*Is everyone one step ahead or am I one step behind? I want to cry, scream. I feel my inner world being pulled in a tug-of-war-type way. Agoraphobia on one side, other aspects of me pulling the other side. I tell myself just keep putting one foot in front of another—it's working! And yet I face another family vacation where I will probably stay home. A prisoner of my own mind. I've been opening the window and had lots of success. I just don't know, think, feel like I'm ready for Catalina Island. I told them it was the place to go—the most fun thing to do. I guess I'll set up "tea" for my pity party.*

*I can hear outside voices saying—just go . . . surely you can push through and go. Even I don't understand why that doesn't work with panic disorder. I just know it's true—that it doesn't help you go. It doesn't help you succeed.*

*Good psychologist ponderings. That ought to keep me in therapy a while longer.*

Journal entry, June 20, 2000
Linda Manassee Buell

# 8 Tips for a Support Person

*"I felt helpless—very much so."*

Debbie Osmond (wife of Donny Osmond)
"48 Hours," CBS Worldwide, August 10, 2000

*"You could see the scare on his face."*

Reuna Campbell (wife of Earl Campbell)
"Rush of Fear," People Magazine, November 4, 1991

*"For me, the causes for a panic attack often don't seem to make sense. From that, I've learned to stop looking for the reasons and offering solutions, no matter how good my intentions are. I've found the best thing I can do is simply to be there for Linda to lean on and allow her to experience it through. I know that she is not the 'panic.' Linda's panic disorder may affect the way we choose some of the activities we do together, but we haven't allowed it to lessen our loving relationship or our commitment to each other."*

Chuck Buell (husband of Linda Manassee Buell)

I wrote this section especially because I am lucky enough to have the most supportive husband in the world. He has stuck with me through thick and thin. He's been with me when I entirely eliminated going to movies, the theatre, sports and other events. He's stayed with me when, at the last minute, I've cancelled our planned vacations and attendances at family events. He's adjusted by vacationing with our sons or his long-time best friend and travelling by himself to be with family during their important times. And he knows how important it is to me that he call and check in with me when he's going to be gone for any length of time.

I can't begin to understand the depth of the frustration, anger and pain these cancellations and my non-participation have caused him, just as he'll never fully understand what it means to have panic disorder. But we both try. For instance, I know that a great deal of his frustration is a result of his feeling helpless. He knows my living with panic and anxiety can sometimes be totally discouraging. I know he wants more than anything to see me not suffer; that he would truly like to make the panic go away.

I'm very lucky. He cares enough to try to learn whatever I can teach him, even when it doesn't always make sense to him. He's willing to listen to how he can help me, which in most cases is nothing more than my just knowing he's around. He understands I need him to call when he's away just to hear his voice.

Panic disorder has significantly changed his life as well as mine. I'm working on trying to understand that and allow him to have his frustrations, and anger and pain. I can't make his feelings go away any more than he can make my panic go away. However, I can create a safe space for him to share his feelings without me getting defensive. I can provide him with information so that he can better understand this disorder. I can continue to let him know the ways in which he can, and has, helped me when I have a panic attack.

Healthy relationships are built on lots and lots of open and honest communication. Start talking and sharing, keep talking and sharing, and don't stop.

# 108

Learn as much as you can about panic disorder. Then also know that you will probably have only about a 75% understanding of the panic anxiety.

# 109

Ask the person with panic disorder to share how they feel, not during a panic attack, but rather when things are calm. Then find out what a panic attack is like for them.

# 110

Just listen; don't try to solve the panic. As much as you may want to, you can't fix it or take away the panic.

# 111

Learn how you can support a person with panic disorder during an attack. It may mean just being there or giving them a hug. Those things can be more supportive than you may ever know.

# 112

Let the person with panic disorder organise some activities that you can do together. You'll be surprised at how much they're willing to try if they can set their own parameters.

# 113

Acknowledge those times when a panic sufferer sincerely says that they want to try to move forward or try activities despite their panic. Your support in this success can encourage them to try again.

# 114

Compromise when possible. Be open to an adjustment that can easily be done that will make the outing successful and more comfortable. Change a departure time to avoid rush hour, take stairs instead of a lift, and make adjustments for other similar activities that are uncomfortable for the person with anxieties.

# 115

Cancel plans under certain circumstances, if necessary. When you do make the decision to cancel, accept that decision and do it without guilt or accusations.

# 116

Share your feelings as a support person. Good two-way communication can go a long way toward helping you both through the tough times.

# 117

Live your own life. At times, it can be painful for the person with panic disorder when you go off to do an activity without them. However, any resentment you may harbour for being held back will only create additional problems.

# 118

Work on keeping your relationship focused on the true person you know and love. Understand that they are going through tough times, and care for them as you would in any other circumstance when they would need your help.

# 119

Seek your own professional counselling. Living with someone with any type of disorder is going to bring up your own emotions and issues.

# 120

Encourage the person with panic disorder to participate in a program for desensitisation. Offer to help them as a buddy to lean on during the initial and tough stages.

# 121

Be a buddy or safe person. Be willing to be gentle and yet a bit firm. Encourage and comfort while helping the person focus on the task at hand. This is a specific role and may not be for everyone.

*Freedom is my capacity to work with the panic energy. Plus not fearing—giving energy—to things we can't control.*

*Panic as a difficulty in my life is there to teach me, have me work with / on, my ability to have patience and compassion with myself.*

Journal entry, September 28, 2001
Linda Manassee Buell

# And Then There Were Hormones

Over the years, I've learned that there are a number of factors that influence my well-being and ability to stay centred and calm. These include getting enough sleep, eating healthy foods, getting regular exercise and minimising stress. I have also monitored my hormonal cycle for years and have recorded an increased level of anxiety just prior to the onset of my monthly cycle.

Just when I thought I was getting all this down, doing well with systematic desensitisation and moving through most of my agoraphobia, I crashed. After not having a panic attack in nearly 16 months, I started to experience multiple panic attacks during a three-month period.

Even with my considerable knowledge of my body's needs, I continued to 'burn the candle at both ends.' For three weeks during a family visit, I didn't eat on an established schedule or pay my usual attention to my food choices. I showed off by doing lots of activities that I hadn't been able to do in the past. I stayed up late to talk with my mother and got up early to get in rounds of golf with my sister. I ignored the stress created by having nine people living in my house instead of just my husband and me.

I did survive the visit without 'panic,' but I noticed how completely exhausted I had become. Even so, I stayed on that demanding, non-stop pace and went ahead with a previously scheduled out-of-town trip. The trip had been designed, in part, as another step of my desensitisation hierarchy. What I couldn't have predicted, however, was the three-hour parking lot stand-still on the freeway due to an overturned semi miles ahead of us. I will say that I was quite proud of myself for not becoming anxious as we crept along ever so slowly at 5 miles per hour toward our destination.

The trip went well—until the second day. I awoke feeling physically miserable, my whole body ached as if I were coming down with the flu and I could barely get out of bed. Then I felt the panic attack coming on. I was hours away from home and I was out of reserves. The trip was no longer fun and we headed home early. I spent the next few days mostly in bed.

I made a conscientious effort to get back to my routines. I was getting back on track and then another series of panic attacks came and went. Now I was confused. I was doing what I was supposed to be doing and it wasn't working. The missing piece was that my changing hormone levels were affecting my reserves, my ability to handle stress, change in diet, and change in sleep.

By this time I was aware of the connection between my anxiety and my monthly cycle. After all, I had tracked and recorded it for years. The problem was I hadn't had a period in quite a few months. In fact for the preceding 10 months, I hadn't been experiencing any regular pattern at all of hormonal changes. My cycles ranged from 17 days to 113 days. Do I think this had an impact on my anxiety and panic disorder and accompanying crashes? Absolutely!

Unfortunately, there haven't been a lot of specific scientific studies done on the relationship of panic disorder and hormonal changes in women. However, according to Dr. Christiane Northrup in her book *The Wisdom of Menopause*, 'There is ample scientific evidence of the brain changes that begin to take place at perimenopause.' She goes on to say, 'Differences in relative levels of oestrogen and progesterone affect the temporal lobe and limbic areas of our brains, and we may find ourselves becoming irritable, anxious, emotionally volatile.'

Now take those brain changes and give them to a person with anxiety or panic disorder and what might you get? Me!

What I suggest and recommend—as with everything else about panic disorder—is to get to know your own body. Read about hormonal changes and see what might apply to you. Talk to your health-care provider about options that incorporate everything you know about yourself and your own body's reaction to these changing hormones. What was recommended to me, for instance, was to take natural hormonal remedies, then hormone replacement therapy, and then the birth control pill. Just as I made my own decision on which, if any, of these options to pursue, you must decide what's best for you.

There are many factors to consider and it is important to find someone who will treat all of you, not just your perimenopause or menopause. You want someone who will help you monitor the changes and adjust accordingly for your body, and you want someone who is knowledgeable about panic and anxiety. Just as some therapists are quick to have a standard answer for treating panic, some doctors have a standard answer for treating perimenopause. This experience is anything but standard.

By the time I go through menopause, the experts will probably have developed even better answers and solutions for panic sufferers including some specific approaches for those who are undergoing perimenopause. Then—as always—it will be up to you and me to research the options, enlist the help of professionals we trust and come to our own conclusions and our own best answers.

# What Is a
# Panic Attack?

*"I think the most important thing to cope with panic or anxiety*
*reaction is your thought. Your thought must be armed with, 'It's OK!*
*I'm not in danger. This panic sensation only means that I am*
*stimulated by something. Remember, I am still alive and have*
*remained well throughout previous experiences, even though I was*
*afraid of dying or going crazy.' "*

Young Hee Choi, M.D.
Associate Professor of Psychiatry,
Seoul Paik Hospital, Inje University (South Korea)

A panic attack occurs when there is a sudden, intense fear or anxiety, or an overwhelming sense of impending doom in the absence of real danger. The attack builds rapidly to its peak, generally within about 10 minutes.

The *American Psychiatric Association: Diagnostic and Statistical Manual of Mental Disorders, Fourth Edition, Text Revision,* says:

The attack is accompanied by four or more of the following physical sensations and psychological reactions:

1. palpitations, pounding heart, or accelerated heart rate
2. sweating

3. trembling or shaking
4. sensations of shortness of breath or smothering
5. feeling of choking
6. chest pain or discomfort
7. nausea or abdominal distress
8. feeling dizzy, unsteady, lightheaded, or faint
9. derealisation (feelings of unreality) or depersonalisation (being detached from oneself)
10. fear of losing control or going crazy
11. fear of dying
12. paraesthesias (numbness or tingling sensations)
13. Chill or hot flushes*

Elke Zuercher-White, Ph.D., states in her book, *An End to Panic: Breakthrough Techniques for Overcoming Panic Disorder*, 'Some people experience other sensations such as sudden diarrhoea, instant headaches, intense weakness or stiffness in the legs, or blurred vision. Research on panic symptoms suggests that three symptoms are particularly common: palpitations, dizziness, and suffocation sensations. As the disorder continues over time, and no physical catastrophe occurs, the fear of going crazy or losing control often becomes the chief fear.'

It only takes seconds for whatever physical symptoms you may experience to begin. These symptoms are caused by a sudden release of various chemicals within your body. Many people experience such intense physical discomfort during an attack that they may think they're having a heart attack or a stoke. However, once you begin calming your body and mind, those chemicals that your body has released will start to dissipate. Whatever your physical sensations may be, they will pass.

*Reprinted with permission from the *Diagnostic and Statistical Manual of Mental Disorders, Fourth Edition, Text Revision.* Copyright 2000 American Psychiatric Association.

Most importantly, remember that while a panic attack or even high anxiety is extremely uncomfortable, it isn't dangerous. You are actually very much in control during an attack and won't do anything crazy, even if it feels like you will. People can and do function through an attack.

Panic is a treatable disorder and early detection for panic disorder can help significantly reduce future potential complications. Plus, a panic attack will not cause you to lose your sanity or have a nervous breakdown. You are *not* going crazy.

Give yourself the gift of getting the help and support you need today!

# Self-Help Books

*An End to Panic: Breakthrough Techniques for Overcoming Panic Disorder, Second Edition* by Elke Zuercher-White, Ph.D. Oakland, CA: New Harbinger, 1998.

*The Anxiety Cure: An Eight-step Program for Getting Well* by Robert L. DuPont, Elizabeth DuPont Spencer and Caroline M. DuPont. New Jersey: John Wiley & Sons, 2003.

*Anxiety Disorders (Wiley Concise Guides to Mental Health)* by Larina Kase, Deborah Roth Ledley and Irving B. Weiner. New Jersey: John Wiley & Sons, 2007.

*Anxiety and Depression Workbook For Dummies, UK Edition* by Elaine Iljon Foreman, Charles H. Elliott, Ph.D. and Laura L. Smith, Ph.D. John Wiley & Sons: West Sussex, 2008.

*The Anxiety and Phobia Workbook, Third Edition* by Edmund J. Bourne, Ph.D. Oakland, CA: New Harbinger, 2000.

*Beyond Anxiety and Phobia: A Step-By-Step Guide to Lifetime Recovery* by Edmund J. Bourne, Ph.D. Oakland, CA: New Harbinger, 2001.

*Embracing the Fear: Learning to Manage Anxiety and Panic Attacks* by Judith Bemis. Center City, MN: Hazelden Information Education, 1994.

*Feel the Fear and Do It Anyway* by Susan Jeffers, Ph.D. New York: Ballantine Books, 2006.

*I'd Rather Laugh: How to Be Happy Even When Life Has Other Plans for You* by Linda Richman. New York: Warner Books, 2001.

*Journey from Anxiety to Freedom: Moving Beyond Panic and Phobias and Learning to Trust Yourself* by Mani Feniger. Roseville, CA: Prima Publishing, 1999.

*Life is Just What You Make It: My Life So Far* by Donny Osmond and Patricia Romanowski. New York: Hyperion, 2006.

*Meditation: A Simple 8-point Program for Translating Spiritual Ideals into Daily Life, Second Edition* by Eknath Easwaran. Tomales, CA: Nilgiri Press, 1993.

*Menopause Made Easy: How to Make the Right Decisions for the Rest of Your Life* by Carolle Jean-Murat, M.D. Carlsbad, CA: Hay House, 1999.

*Overcoming Anxiety For Dummies, UK Edition* by Elaine Iljon Foreman, Charles H. Elliott, Ph.D. and Laura L. Smith, Ph.D. West Sussex: John Wiley & Sons, 2007.

*Panic Free: Eliminate Anxiety/Panic Attacks Without Drugs and Take Control of Your Life* by Lynne Freeman, Ph.D. Sherman Oaks, CA: Arden Books, 1999.

*Perimenopause: Changes in Women's Health After 35, Second Edition* by L. Darlene Lanka, M.D., James E. Huston, M.D. and Lois Jovanovic. Oakland, CA: New Harbinger Publications, 2001.

*Phobia Free: A Medical Breakthrough Linking 90% of All Phobias & Panic Attacks to a Hidden Physical Problem* by Harold N. Levinson and Steven Carter. New York: Fine Communications, 1999.

*Potatoes Not Prozac* by Kathleen DesMaisons, Ph.D. and Candace B. Pert, Ph.D. New York: Simon & Schuster, 1999.

*Prescription for Nutritional Healing, Fourth Edition* by Phyllis A. Balch, C.N.C. and James F. Balch, M.D. New York: Avery Penguin Putnam. 2006.

*Triumph Over Fear* by Jerilyn Ross (President of the Anxiety Disorders Association of America). New York: Bantam Books, 1994.

*Triumph Over Shyness: Conquering Shyness & Social Anxiety* by Murray B. Stein, M.D. and John R. Walker, Ph.D. New York: McGraw-Hill, 2003.

*Wherever You Go There You Are: Mindfulness Meditation in Everyday Life* by Jon Kabat-Zinn. New York: Hyperion, 1995.

*The Wisdom of Menopause: Creating Physical and Emotional Health and Healing During the Change, Second Edition* by Christiane Northrup. M.D. New York: Bantam Books, 2006.

# Other Resources

**Anxieties.com**
www.anxieties.com

**Anxiety Care**
www.anxietycare.org.uk

**The Anxiety Disorder Association of America**
www.adaa.org

**Anxiety Disorder Resource Centre**
www.anxiety-uk.org

**Anxiety Matters**
www.anxietymatters.com

**The Anxiety and Panic Internet Resource (TAPIR)**
www.algy.com/anxiety

**The British Association of Behavioural and Cognitive Psychotherapies**
www.babcp.com

## The British Psychological Society
St Andrews House
48 Princess Road East
Leicester LE1 7DR
+44 (0)116 254 9568
www.bps.org.uk

## Centre for Anxiety Disorders and Trauma
99 Denmark Hill
London SE5 8AF
020 3228 2101
http://psychology.iop.kcl.ac.uk/cadat/

## Freedom From Fear
www.freedomfromfear.com

## The Department of Health
Richmond House
79 Whitehall
London SW1A 2NS
020 7210 4850
www.dh.gov.uk

## Internet Mental Health
www.mentalhealth.com

## Mental Health Foundation
9th Floor
Sea Containers House
20 Upper Ground
London SE1 9QB
United Kingdom
020 7803 1101
www.mentalhealth.org.uk

**Mind**
www.mind.org

**National Institute for Health and Clinical Excellence**
www.nice.org.uk/guidance/index.
jsp?action=byID&r=true&o=10960

**National Institute of Mental Health for England**
www.nimhe.csip.org.uk

**National Mental Health Association**
www.nmha.org

**National Phobics Society**
www.phobics-society.org.uk

**Net Doctor**
www.netdoctor.co.uk/diseases/depression/anxietydisorders_
000017.htm

**No More Panic**
www.nomorepanic.co.uk

**No Panic**
www.nopanic.org.uk

**Obsessive-Compulsive Foundation**
www.ocfoundation.org

**The Panic Center**
www.paniccenter.net

**Panic Support 4 U**
www.panicsupport4u.com

**Phobics-Awareness**
www.phobics-awareness.org

**PsychiatryMatters.MD**
http://psychiatrymatters.md

**PsychNet-UK**
www.psychnet-uk.com

**Wallsend Self Help Group**
www.wshg.org.uk

# About The Author

L   inda Manassee Buell, MCC, is a Master Certified Coach, a
     Certified Professional Mentor Coach and a Group Coach-
     ing Specialist. She is the founder and owner of Simplify
Life (www.simplifylife.com), a professional lifestyle coaching
company that helps people create the life they truly desire.

For the last twelve years, Linda has personally coached hun-
dreds of people both individually and in groups across the United
States, as well as in England, Russia, Israel, Lebanon, and Japan
to help them start their own businesses, define their career desires
and simplify their lives. Linda is also a successful author of a
series of Simplify Your Life audiotapes and books. Prior to all that,
she spent 17 years in upper management with a major Fortune
500 Company. Over the last fifteen years, she has been a public

speaker and media spokesperson and is often interviewed and quoted as an expert in the field of life simplification by US newspapers and television and radio stations.

Linda experienced her first major panic attack in the summer of 1992. She didn't know that she had panic disorder with agoraphobia until 1994, when her therapist informed her of the diagnosis. She first experienced cognitive behavioural therapy for panic disorder as part of a 12-week group programme shortly thereafter. Years later, after leaving her corporate job and relocating twice to other cities, Linda found that her agoraphobia was growing and taking over large portions of her life. She added the benefits of virtual reality technology in combination with traditional cognitive behavioural therapy to start working through the agoraphobia. With good nutrition, meditation, yoga, personal coaching, and continued systematic desensitisation, she is successfully living the life she loves. Calling herself a 'recovering' agoraphobic, Linda recently relocated to Colorado and is pleased to report that she actually travelled by plane for the first time in over 10 years and has had no recurrence of the previous agoraphobic symptoms in moving to a new city. She is now enjoying life in the Denver area with her husband, Chuck.

*"It is an authentic reality that we can actually live and play in the life we generally just dream about. This truth is solidly evident to me as I am living my dream life today. To help others find and live theirs is why I created my business, 'Simplify Life.' "*

Linda Manassee Buell

MS 15

Printed and bound in the UK by
CPI Antony Rowe, Eastbourne